# WRONG SIDE OF TOWN

First published in 2015 by
The Dedalus Press
13 Moyclare Road
Baldoyle
Dublin 13
Ireland

www.**dedaluspress**.com

Editor: Pat Boran

ISBN 978 1 910251 09 6

Dedalus Press titles are represented in the UK by
Central Books, 99 Wallis Road, London E9 5LN
and in North America by Syracuse University Press, Inc.,
621 Skytop Road, Suite 110, Syracuse, New York 13244.

Cover photograph © Linea | Dreamstime.com

The Dedalus Press receives financial assistance from
The Arts Council / An Chomhairle Ealaíon

# WRONG SIDE OF TOWN

## Aidan Murphy

**DEDALUS PRESS**
DUBLIN, IRELAND

## ACKNOWLEDGEMENTS

Thanks are due to the editors of the following publications in which a number of these poems, or versions of them, originally appeared:

*A Miscellany of Irish Poetry* (Shanghai Literature); *Best Irish Poetry 2010; Poetry International; Poetry Ireland Review; Southword; The Irish Examiner; The Irish Independent; The SHOp; What We Found There: Irish Poets Respond to the Treasures of the National Museum (ed. Theo Dorgan)* and *The Sunday Tribune.*

The author gratefully acknowledges The Arts Council of Ireland and the Trustees of the Patrick and Katherine Kavanagh Poetry Fellowship for invaluable assistance.

# Contents

☙

☙

*In Memory of Dolly (Mary) Murphy*

"In the movies of my childhood the heroes
after skilled wordplay and moral victories
leave with absolutely nothing
to do for the rest of their lives."
— Michael Ondaatje

# Mr. Sardonicus

Nearby the graveyard gate
under the streetlight at dusk
I related the tale of the sinister man
whose face was so hideous
the sight of it killed the beholder.
He had flesh from his brow to his eyebrows,
but white skullbone from eyes to chin:
Mr. Sardonicus — phantom with a rictus grin.

It was pitchdark when I finished my tale,
moth-flurries banging on the metal hood
of the weak light above us,
random sizzlings on the hot bulb as we sneaked
away into the empty gardens — unheard
by adults tuned to the latest from the Bay of Pigs —
cutting a furtive path to a neighbour's shed
to peer into the glassy eyes
of fox furs hung from rusty nails.

# The Wolf Man

I remember the wolf man
who lived up the lane
with his roly-poly wife
and their three timid cubs.
He drove a Volks.
He doffed his cap
respectful of 'the gentler sex',
and though I never understood
his jokes, the neighbors said
he was the funniest of folks.

I'll never forget the night he turned,
though whether the moon
was full I can't recall,
only the terror, the rancid
spirit-taste of his long
salivating tongue,
his strong teeth
grinding against mine.

# Death, Our Neighbour

Death was in our street when Spring was in full bloom.
He wore a black homburg, walked with a spiny stick,
smiled as he hitched up the knees of his elegant suit
to squat with us on kerbs, pulling cards from sleeve and boot.
But all too soon our elders brought us to his prayer-
hushed room to kneel and view the waxy face, the hands
set like blancmange, the starched blue cuffs empty of tricks

# Quartet

*in memory of Patrick Galvin*

My mother enjoyed your brief company.
She connected with your plainspeak
about the rugged citizens of poor
Dunbar and Margaret Streets,
the burdensome travails of shoeless Cork.
For a time she stood her signed copy
of *Song for a Poor Boy*
in a place of honour,
in the glass cabinet in the front room.
And though she doesn't remember you now,
or me, or anyone else for that matter,
she used to post me newspaper clippings
of those rare milestones
of your late comeback.

I recall, after the opening night
of *The Burning of Bridget Cleary,*
long hours of wine and gin in Wynn's Hotel,
you, me and Colette, me
yapping nonstop about vintage film,
reducing you to almost-tears
with tales of classic schmaltz —
Stella Dallas, Mildred Pierce, Madame X —
until we said our late, moist-eyed goodnights.
And your phonecall the following day —
"Murphy, don't ever do that to me again."

Paddy,
how many madwomen of Cork were there?
I think I saw at least a dozen
spinning in circles at moonlit crossroads,
and I heard of many others who went missing,
"bad with the nerves," they'd say.
The blight was all around us
and I too jumped the boat across the water.
But, unlike you,
I never found Christ in London;
though I searched real hard.

Did I dream it
or did your spirit
pillow my shoulders
with steady palms
and did I hear
your flat Cork lilt
inside my ear:
Beware the trickery of the sun,
your enemies will come
dressed as comrades,
be doggy wide.

# If I Were Cary Grant

We're trapped, old girl, inside this airless room.
The temperature's unbearable and rising;
the water-level's inching past our waists.
And as an added bonus, just in case,
a sly explosive's primed to detonate.

If I were Cary Grant, sweet heart,
I'd spy above us in the nick of time
a ventilator, a miraculous door.
Then stooping low, I'd coax you,
in a baritone as smooth
as pebbles rolling to a shore,
to step up pronto on my manly back.

But you and I, my dear,
we're reels beyond the glitzy
swindles of the dream-makers,
the candy sunsets of the ad-men.
The best this ending will allow us
is a swift exploding into random
bloody pieces of each other;
before we burn, or suffocate, or drown.

# Sisters in Exile

From Sunbeam, Douglas and the Blarney woollen mills
they earned the price of the boat.
The luckier ones had buttons to spare
as they sailed away,
their harried, nervous faces
diminished in the sheet-faced mob
waving scarves from the upper decks.
Homes would be morgues without them.
Halls would grieve for the clacking of high heels.
Stairs would lament for the shuffling of slippers.
Beds would pine for basking magazines,
gossip and the lazy steam of cocoa mugs.

They sent back letters on scented paper —
violet, lavender, thin as onion skin.
Postcards that unscrolled like unbuttoned accordions
with technicolour views of Toronto, Seattle, New York.
They sent clothes left by hotel guests they skivvied for —
hipsters, jeans, polo-shirts and eye-blinding jumpers.
They sent Dell and Marvel comics and Polaroids
of the marvels they had become — wondrous strangers
with beehives, tight sweaters, checkered slacks,
leaning on the fenders of pastel Cadillacs,
framed by sky-stabbing towers.

But their lives were far from glamorous.
In truth they were skinned to the bone from work and rent,
living on processed cheese, tinned ham and powdered milk,
saving every hard-earned cent
for the short-lived leisure of a Sunday dance.

# On the Demolition of The Arcadia Ballroom, Cork

The ghosts of the waltzing revellers are no match
for the bankers' bullies and their agents, so
shaking the dust from their Sunday best
they stagger from the ruins and wander
in pairs towards Kent Station.
Some head south and some head north;
a couple float Chagall-like
over the abandoned mills;
the rest dance into the city centre
to foxtrot in the hollow shopping malls,
or take their shoes off to recline
on the steps of The Capitol Cineplex —
their spirits fading into summer's end.

# Motherlove

"You'll never be pinned down," she said,
"and your joinedup eyebrows tell me
your heart is full of deceit."

She always spoke to me that way,
in symbols, portents,
mysterious cocoons
that never hatched
and tried my patience.

She smelled of talc and lemon,
and her skin was like cream in sunlight.
But what smelled best was the sweat
on the hairs peeking out of her underarms,
between the slip-straps of her green summer dress.

# What's Keeping You?

What's keeping you?

I have polished my speech to a deep black shine
and my neighbourly bell is dying to chime,
but my gate never creaks and the day goes quickly dark.

What's keeping you?

Each hollow day you are not here
is filled with sleep and slaughtered time,
and the news from the world outside
is downcast, loud with mishaps.

What's keeping you?

I close my eyes and pray
it's nothing worse than change of mind,
but who will ever know me
if you never come?

# The Gravity of Money

I crammed
my pockets with stones,
my make-believe money.

With hands rooted deep
I rattled my fists full
of pebbles, making louder

more important jangling
than the meagre coppers
in my father's trousers;

or I tied sand-filled
jute bags to my belt,
like a burro bearing gold dust,

so heavy I could barely waddle
while my father quick-marched,
head high, stony broke.

# Lullaby

*for Frank on his 60ᵗʰ*

Mother,
when I grow up
I want to be
an Ant Watcher
a Wave Checker
a Sky Glazier
a Shadow Timer
a Leaf Counter
a Dream Filter
a Grass Layer
a Straw Chewer
a Moon Washer.

Son,
when you grow up
you'll get a job
and go to work
and be a man
just like your father.

Mother,
what is a man?

Hush child,
go to sleep now.

# Wrong Side of Town

It was the wrong side of town for pedestrians.
Classic motors took up every inch of kerb space —
nifty cream models upholstered in suede,
blood-red hotrods with detachable rooftops;
a prideful display of virility in chrome.

It was the wrong side of town for poor dressers.
Unhealthy in your hand-me-downs you ambled
in on a traffic of bodies dressed to impress.
Cosmeticized creatures in silver and gold
slipped demurely into taxicabs.
                                    Senile codgers
winking in the windows of *The Club Elite*
flashed lasered creases, snowcapped teeth.

There was no one you knew
among the retouched faces.
No one you knew
in the lava-lamp-lit doorway of The Bamboo Palace.
No one you knew
muttering prayers and salutations to the parking-meters.
No one you knew
drooling the blues into a banged-up *Hohner*.

It was the wrong side of town for a green trusting boy.
From your first step over the line you were under the radar
tracked by the heat of an eye ever-looking
for someone obtrusive like you,
foolhardy as Christ on the wrong side of town.

# J's Elegy

I see you again in Cork's first nightclub
tossing back overpriced plonk and
hassling the DJ for *Roxy* and *Sparks*,
or talking shite with ladies of the night
from Merseyside and Lancashire,
in your yellow stretch-pants and moth-eaten fur,
sporting the weathered fez that made you
look about as Turkish as Stan Laurel.
Later, when the bouncers shovel the revellers streetwards,
you will be dead drunk in a red vinyl booth.
In the end they'll have to carry you out,
underarm, stiff as a plank,
and drop you down deadweight
next to the overspilling litter bins,
where I will wait for hours beside you
for a driver crazy enough to bear you safely home.

# AWOL

On those nights when I went missing
you might have found me
in the backside of Burger King
or in some bar on Barrack Street
with the ghost of Mick McQuaid,
his left hand holding an antique scales,
his right banging coins into a rusted till;

or later in some garish karaoke lounge
wearing the clothes of a stranger,
shoulder to shoulder with imminent danger
solid as a hammer but ready
in a minute to be smoke
if anyone got close.

# The Millionaires' Club

The Millionaires' Club is a moveable feast.
You might find it
down the ass-end of a seedy alley
or atop a marble staircase,
in a blooming country garden
soundtracked by a cool amalgam
of grasshoppers fiddling and fingers
sprinkling sugar over strawberries,
or along forgotten roads beside
the ruined ghosts of gas stations.
You won't find it in your Lonely Planet
or on your Google Earth,
it's off the radar, lost
to GPS and satellite.
In The Millionaires' Club
your fat wallet wields no clout.
It cares little for your flashy motorcades,
your art, your property or tailor,
dealing only in currencies
that shapeshift like quicksilver.

# Stuff

*for Humphrey*

When it's time for a change
you forget
that things are sometimes
better undisturbed.

Do one room
you're compelled to do another;
decorating gathers momentum
like fastforward tape.

The new floor mocks the wall;
the brackets misfit and mismatch;
the ceiling looks drab
like never before;

so you rearrange again,
shift portions of the past,
but you can't stay uninvolved
like some paid removal man

and stuff,
buried for years,
creeps up from behind
and roots you to the spot.

There's no end to it:
no final sorting.
That chair, that rug,
that bracelet from the blue,

old letters, keys
and photographs —
the surprising paraphernalia
of life will hound you.

# The Nets of Tradition

I tore the nets down from the porthole windows —
the ancient yellow nets that almost powdered in my hands —
and let the sunlight in upon the Irish Wolfhound
basking on the greasy lino since the Civil War
who turned instantly to dust and blew away.

But the woman of the house was not well-pleased.
She ordered that the nets be laundered and re-hung
to gather grit and grime another century.

# Leonard Cohen at the Royal Hospital, Dublin

Doffing a cool blue fedora, he comes
graciously from the shadows.
With the delicate face
of a merchant rich in melancholy,
with his famous, brazen grin
he bows us in;
and we go willingly
like children to kindness,
into his storm
of redemption and loss,
into the smoky voice
of the one-and-only
truly kosher
*Grocer of Despair* —
a man with nothing to sell but song
that pulls the triggers of our hearts
and moistens the cratered lips of the moon.


*14/06/08*

# Bastille Day, Dublin 2009

In airy Georgian rooms ablaze with crystal light
the A-list celebs and the platinum hards
gather tonight to honour the bards.

After the hugging
the air-kissing and the schmoozing
comes the toasting
and the fawning and the boasting,
followed by the drinking and the dancing,
the heaping on of laurel leaves,
the dishing of the dirt.

The celebrations close down after sunrise;
the city's sunlit bridges
eclipsed by hooded beggars.

# Cyrano in Dublin

I write verses for the hard men who can't read or write.
Sentimental endearments for blind grannies,
quirky haikus for closet trannies.
Verses for mothers and brothers in jail,
verses for the Best Dads in the World out on bail.
All for a meagre few bob and a couple of rounds,
and never an unkind word about my *youknowwhat.*

# Takeover

We were expecting a grand affair:
a sleek black window-tinted limousine;
a strident welcoming fanfare.
Three cheers at least, followed by
traditional rhetoric, robust handshakes.

But when it came, it came
unceremoniously: a shapeless
conundrum of cables, wires and bubblewrap
bound in plastic in a box
in the back of a nondescript van.

Then, under cover of the witching hour
without a solitary witness,
with the flick of a switch
installed in power.

# Rogues

"I love a rogue," she said,
and I concurred.
To me they were the blossoms
of the bunch,
those handsome rogues
with sincere eyes
and trusting handclasps.

Oh yes! We gave
our households and our hearts
away to flashy rogues, who lit
the dull flat beltway of our days.

"What fools we were," I said,
and she agreed.
It didn't turn out as we believed.
The rogues were rogues indeed,
who pinched the pounds
of hope we'd saved
based on their charming words
and honeyed deeds.

# A Lifestyle

In Beirut in '84, she was highly praised and prized for her
    close mouth
when she carried those sensitive parcels from house to house.
After that, she spied in Tehran for a spell, transmitting
top-level info that was duly scanned and shredded — Then
*Poof!* — She vanished in thin air like Keyser Soze, until
a chance glance clocked her in Dubai, cavorting
in a penthouse pool with spooks and billionaires,
iridescent on MDMA.
She was — unsurprisingly — reeled in. And then
cast out again as a sex-fuelled marionette,
to do the state some service on her back.
The alternative was a posting to Tijuana to pack cocaine
in a sweaty warehouse, in underwear and surgical mask.
She's out to pasture now. Passing her twilight days
sewing dissident slogans on clothing for teens
in between marathon bouts of XBox.

# Black Rose

Night after night he un-nerved her with vile rumours
of Blacks and A-Rabs and Islamers
who would soon be taking over
bringing with them crime and terror.

Of fragile mind she was easily deceived,
easily swayed by the force of his bigotry,
so she followed him south to a brandnew house
on the coast of an all-white colony.

There he pottered to his heart's content
in a private Eden of his dreams
with his trellised ivy, his skull-clipped hedge
and his Flymo gleaming in his pale pine shed,

while she languished in a wheelchair
under triple-glazed locked windows
pining for the gossip of the washing line
and the life she left behind on neighbourly stairwells.

He buried her with minimum fuss —
a perfunctory washing of hands —
never guessing she would spring back soon
from the bleached heart of his Aryan blooms
in the shape, as if to spite him, of a robust black rose.

# Taxi

Last night I took a taxi in the rain;
sat in the back in the sour
scent of puke and musky aftershave.

The moment we pulled out
the driver began a tirade
about the foreigners
out to steal our women and his trade.

Did I have to listen to this?
I was tired, somewhat pissed,
so I took it and tuned out.

Cost me less in the end.
"Six euro to you," he said,
tipping me a tribal wink
as if we were lifelong friends.

# Crash

A fierce crush of metal brings me to the window:
two shattered cars, a pond of broken glass
and plastic spattered dark with blood.
Above the luscious trees the swept blue
guarantees another day of rare heat, so
I take a beer and sandwich to the stoop and wait
among the gatherers in summer light
for the whooping ambulances. Here
are faces I've not seen in months,
the ashen faces of bedsit tenants,
the screwed-down faces of child-mothers
and the prematurely old faces of their doll-like broods,
the drug-glinting faces of outpatients
in threadbare gowns and slippers,
the ominous masks of tragedy gourmets.
Over walls and hedges strangers pass comments to strangers,
their words imbued with an importance that elevates them,
momentarily, above drudgery and loneliness.
Talking for the sake of talking.
Dreading the silence when the sirens go.

# Minor Offences

Out of the traffic's sight beneath the old woman's window
the kids gang up at nightfall.
They light fires of fag boxes, lolly sticks, chocolate wrappers,
scream out nicknames and obscenities and carve into the bricks
initials of their fragile selves and momentary lusts.
Alone inside the woman fidgets at the table,
kneads the sweat between her clasped hands,
and at the sound of bottles breaking
her loose skin tenses in terror.
She turns the telly up real loud to some trashy American
    thriller
full of fucks, gunfire and demolitions,
until she cannot hear a thing outside:
no more violent shouts or breakages,
not even the tenant upstairs banging,
banging his displeasure with his boot upon the floor.

# Smoker's Epitaph

Here lies
'Topper for the Road'
shrouded in his best
brown smoking smock
who fell from grace
from Turkish Slims
to Black Sobranie
from Halfzware Shag
to Blonde Virginia
then
right
on
down
to Pale Light Flake
that scorched like thatch
but never once succumbed
to the draw of the Nicotine Patch.

# Speed Date

"Did you ever have
sex, so good,
so intense,
you wanted to
kill, or eat
your partner?"

Me and my big mouth ...

When the awkward silence dies —
which takes forever —
she asks to be excused.

I wait.

Our foamy coffees
shrink to stone-cold scum.
Our chocolate sponge cakes
capsize into pools of cream.

I don't think she's coming back.

*"Fetch me your drugs, Art of Poetry,*
*that make one unaware,*
*for a while, of the wound."*
—CP Cavafy, *Melancholy of Jason*

*I sing the body unconscious*
*black pillows of sleep*

*the beautiful blackout*
*that masticates our fears*

*the hours of blissful zero*
*that cauterize all wounds*

# Invocation

Come now, Poembeast,
here is the menu you drool for:

The carcass opened up,
the rib-sheets aired;

the heart sliced into chewy ribbons
wet with tears;

the bile-spiced cuts
already festering;

the blood, the marrow of the bone
made sweet with sorrow.

# Your Ear

And in the utter darkness of my desolation
Lo & Behold! I am visited by your ear

that smartly folds itself in half, flaps open
and shut like the ravenous mouth of a fledgling,

between whose mutant lips I spoon
the loving words I meant for you;

now I wait for your sighs of gratitude,
your great shudders of satisfaction.

# Basic Alchemy

A pinch of this,
a grain of that:
I'm mixing cocktails
in the den, attempting
to correct imbalances.

I shake and drain,
I drip and grind; but I'm
no Victor Frankenstein
trying to unlock
the mysteries of life
and death.

        I'm just
another urban warlock
in a Nike baseball cap
who wants to be happy
for one whole day.

# Futility

I called her Futility,
my screwed-up Muse.

She was smart as a whip
at the start. Then she stopped

dressing and sat in my lap
for days, asleep on my shoulder.

I didn't even try to get up, blessed
in the comfort of her dead weight.

## The Prisoner

The prisoner has a skeleton key,
a satnav of the tunnels,
a chart of the path to the free world.

He has the guards in his pocket,
a customized car beyond the wall
primed to go,

and a loyal woman waiting
in a hotel with a bag
brimming over with cash.

Still, the prisoner stays put:
moving only from cell to shower
to yard back to cell,
perplexing the warden.

# Accidental Blood

Last night
I came home
bloodstained.
As I was running
for the last tram
I went down
on my right side,
grazed fingers,
knuckles, hip
and elbow;
nothing serious.

I ran a bath.
I soaked
in liquid heat
for half an hour.
How good it felt
after a long night
on the town to be
washing off
blameless,
shameless,
accidental blood.
How wonderful
not to wake
this morning with
a plum-bruised eye
or broken nose.

# Watchman

Had I choice I would have chosen
to march south with the others;
but I was ordered to remain

here in this concrete, whitewashed square,
in the middle of this torched field,
in this windowless box

with the twitching snout
of a close-circuit lens clamped
high above a padlocked door

keeping watch on the flatscreen frontier,
bones flying to dust, flesh
falling to ghosts on the monitor.

# Skiing Lesson

When the going down is smooth
they will be dying to save you —

the white slopes black with stickmen
and St. Bernards bearing brandy.

But when you hit the jagged teeth
that bite and slice you into strips

none will be there to marvel at
the vivid bloody rags upon the snow.

# The New Republic of Despair

At 4.30 in the afternoon —
the dingy sieves on the windows
straining the dregs of daylight —
she brings him chips and tea.

It snowed, she says, this morning,
near two smooth inches in the yard
before the day awoke and churned
its purity to slush.

She switches on the TV set,
towels his sweat-stale flesh
then leaves him gazing at the screen,
at men in mourning for redundant hands,
the camera clawing at their desperate eyes.

# Appetite

Food doesn't really bother me.
I don't do dinner easily

or lunch much better.
But don't ever mistake me

for a man with no appetite.
My brain is a glutton, obese

from the gristle of word and vision.
And I have days when I could eat

the planet: its outers, its innards,
every tasty, rancid crumb.

# Things Go Better with Anaesthetic

Sick at heart I lumber to The Boardwalk Candy Store
for something sweet to take the edge away.
Back home I gorge myself empty, then curl
for days in a space not riddled with tremors
where one day morphs into another
and the clock's hands circle with graceful motion.

# Those Black Ballads

Ours is a sordid tale, best forgotten,
but those black ballads won't let us.
Seeding in strangers' mouths
they pursue us into the woods
and across bright morning cities,
bearing deadly spores and dropping
incantations from dark places where
surgeons operate with rusty nails
and love breaks knees with hammers.

## Black Rhino

Not tonight, my love.
I am going outside to hide in the bushes
because that dangerous cloud is passing
through me, and my bile is rising.

Even here my skin is bristling; as I watch
the antics of the drunken guests
behind the patio glass,
I have to hold myself from charging.

Best now to head up to the house
I secretly built in the hills, where
I can steam without burning.

# Vulture

That ugly
dirty bird
on the branch
of that burnt-out tree
is me
      following
the fresh stench of offal
preening my gravy feathers
peering crosseyed at the earth
for red bursts of exploitation.

# In the Reptile House

I will never be cold again.
Here in my skin
with my slithery fiends
I exult in captivity.
Prince of the pit!
King of the coil!
Warm in my nest
and milked of venom.

# Elephant Skull

Here is a strange grail indeed!
A Cyclopean vessel with teeth,
a ponderous mass
bereft of flesh and ivory.

What monstrous apparition
imbibed from this gargantuan mug
to leave it so parched

with a thirst
that all the world's tears —
past, present and to come —
will never slake?

# 1st Poet in Space

Laika the ghost-dog
guides me around.

She shows me the burnt-out
souls toppling earthwards
trailing ash and dust.

She points at galaxies combusting,
Möbius-strips aflame spiraling outwards
shrieking like outraged women.

I beg not to see any more
but the bitch is insistent:
she clamps my leg in her spectral jaw
and in spite of my pleas
drags me onwards.

# Malice Aforethought

Last time they met she killed him
discreetly, with words
perfected to a spear
no heart could bear.
But no one saw her lips move.
No one witnessed
the light clicking off in his eyes
or the onset of his fatal weariness.
And later when she heard
the news of his demise
she even had the gall
to feign a shocked surprise.

# Yet

Colder than a barrel of iced fish
       Yet
My organs melt at the sight of you

Hate you with a diamond will
       Yet
Can't stop conjuring the shape of you

Harder than a double fist
       Yet
Await your blows with an exultant heart.

# Strange Truce

From feet to crown
we zipped each other
upside down.
What spilled out
was unpleasant
to the nose and eye,
yet strangely
brought us nearer
to this present,
face to face
without a word
or stir of unease,
burned to the wick
of wit's end.

# Why Can't You Let Me Stay Broken?

Anxious, you stay up all night
ruining your sight
consulting textbooks of malaise;

but whenever you track down
an illness that matches my symptoms
my sickness slides into another zone.

Why can't you let me stay broken?
Why can't you end your well-intentioned probing?
Stop singing me out of my coma, and bury me,
bruises and all, deep in neutral waters.

# The School of Slowing Down

There are no teachers here.
No one to beat or abuse me.
No one to condemn or choose me.
The contour of my body
is wrapped in sensor wire
and the shallow waves of time
lap round my flesh
shorting me circuit by circuit.
I am beginning to understand
what little remains
what little power is left.
Easing my foot from the accelerator.
Learning to brake.

# The Strategy for Getting By

Forget everything you know and learn
to talk about anything at all.
In this way
the volume of your thought
will retreat to mute
and your heart will beat
on auto-pilot.
This condition —
you daren't call it *Life*,
existence at best, endurance at worst —
will carry you
from street to street
from hour to hour
over the hurdles of empty pockets
over the snares of duplicitous earth.

## Situation Wanted

Can anybody use an experienced Agent Provocateur?
A man with a predilection for destruction
and a skill for concocting unease?

How about you, my slyboot Government?
Surely you can use someone who knows
the weakest places of the heart,
the links where humankind is most pliable?

Surely you could plant me deep
in wholesome communities?
Wind me up and let me wreak
my natural havoc?

# Showdown with the King of Sorrow

I know you. I've seen
that blue-black crown before.
You are the king of sorrow,
the monarch of grief,
the potentate of despair
in your cascading robes
of fears and tears,
staring at me from the bathroom mirror.
Draw close to me. Come closer still
until we're eye to eye, until I feel
the weeping of your finery
damp against my cheap sweatshirt,
until I strike first with my fist
and leave you smashed — in jagged
jigsaw pieces on the bathroom floor.

# A Little Resurrection

A little bit more …
he whacks at the wall,
he scrapes the dirt with his fingers.

Not too far now …
impelled by longdistance
memories of light
he's getting warmer,
his bones cracking, thawing.

And that slow throbbing in his ear?
Could it be
the timid beating
of a heart not fully broken?

# New Clothes

The sweetest craziest woman he knows
is putting on new clothes.
The crisp white outfit
suits the purpose in her eyes,
the way she moves among the crowds,
capable, serene,
as he stalks her for the final time
down to the bridge that marks
the county line where roads diverge.
There he pauses, blowing
a kiss she will never receive,
wishing that no more shadows
will follow or foul her.

# Broken Necklace

The clasp of my will is broken
yet still I rejoice.

I was so weary
of its stubborn single-mindedness,
its fixed tedium.

Now, see how
it glisters on the rug
like scrambled landing-lights:
A luminous trail of busted beads.

# Guardian Angel

She could have kicked me out
in snow in rain and cold,
but she was never one to raise
a foot, a hand, even an eyebrow
to any man or woman
on the far side of luck.

Instead she eased me out
with stealth, the long fingers
of her left hand on my shoulderbone,
her right index finger pointing
upwards to the fleecy clouds —
her merciful trickery diverting
my gaze from the vortex below.

# The Grip

You advise me to let go;
thanks, but no thanks.
Don't get me wrong: I know
the tight holds we keep
on family and friends,
on lovers, dogs and cats,
may bring us nothing more
than grief and wrath.

But when I watched my girl
get sucked back up the waterslide
and disappear, I let her go;

and when I watched my boy
slouch through an ill-lit gauntlet
of barbarians, I let him go;

and when I saw myself
get cynical and hard while plummeting
from parapets of sense, I let me go.

Too much. Too much letting go.
From here I swear

on dead friends' eyes, to grip.
The whole grip.
Nothing but the grip.